WHY ME?

There is a positive aspect

to the question too…

Kayode + Gbemi
Asiola
Always Be Positive
Vanessa cel
25.02.22

Lola Oyebade

Great Nation
Publishing House
Transforming the minds

Why Me? *There is a positive aspect to the question too...*

First published in Great Britain in 2022 by Great Nation Publishing House Ltd

Great Nation Publishing House Ltd
Suite 9,
6 Union Street,
Luton LU1 3AN
England

Tel: +44 (0) 203 488 4807
Email: info@gnpublishinghouse.com

Book cover design: josephademosu01@gmail.com
Typeset and page layout design: josephademosu01@gmail.com

ISBN: 978-1-908259-20-2

CONTENTS

DEDICATION

This book is dedicated to all my brethren who in the course of their service to the King have had to ask this important question. If you have not got to the stage of asking "Why me?", the book is written to help you understand the positive side to that question.

Thank you for reading and learning.

ACKNOWLEDGEMENT

To my brethren in the faith of our Lord and Saviour Jesus Christ, I acknowledge the blessing that all of you are in, and your stand for truth in your nation.

Your sacrifices for your belief in Christ and your stand against opposing forces are all nothing compared to the reward that awaits us all when we get HOME in Heaven.

I also appreciate the lives of men and women raised by God to pray for me in intense warfare and at different seasons. All your prayers for me have tremendous power as mine is for you too. Thank you for not breaking ranks but for standing shoulder to shoulder with me. You know yourselves as the Lord knows you.

Finally, to my HOTRIC Family, you are special! Thank you for not compromising the word of God but allowing the process to continue till Christ is formed in us. We are not there yet but we are sure not where we used to be!

ENDORSEMENTS

"An interesting and intriguing book. Why me? So often we focus on the negative aspect of this question without realising that there is a positive aspect to it and when we find that positive aspect we should lose ourself in worship to God out of a heart of gratitude"

Margaret Bankole

Pastor Lola has touched another raw nerve in the Body Christ: always asking God, "Why me?" when things don't align with our expectations. She is calling us to rephrase the question, "Why not me?" if indeed we are people of faith and are assured of the love of God for us. Thank you for stirring the hornet's nest again with the aim of making us realize that "...all things work together for good for them that love God and are the called according to His purpose" (Rom.8:28).

Tunde Ogedengbe
Lead Pastor
Kingdom Arena, Luton, UK.

INTRODUCTION

One of the most asked questions by anyone in a time of crisis is "Why me?".

We ask this question when we receive bad news of any kind or when we hear unexpected news that seems to have no end (because it looks like there's no end to it!).

We ask this question when it seems like there's no end to pain; and disaster is all we see. Like Job in the Bible, we sometimes experience constant news that barrages our mind and we seat with frustration and ask "Why me?".

We ask this question when those we trusted betray us and it seems no one will believe our side of events.

But in this book you are about to find out the positive side to that question "Why me?".

When you are blessed beyond your expectation, you will also realise "Why me?". When you have a job and your children return home from their outings safely, they get married and bear you grandchildren, you should ask "Why me?".

When you have a roof over your head and are breathing normally without medical assistance, you should ask "Why me?".

The list is endless; and, I pray that this book will help address your understanding of why the question should not only be seen as necessary in crisis but also in good times.

To ask "Why me?" in troubled times, you should also ask "Why me?" in good times too, as there are many who desire to have what you've got!

Chapter One
What's going on?

On the afternoon of Sunday, 22nd September 1991, when I returned home from our church's first service to rest and get ready for the week starting Monday, as I got on my bed, I heard a knock on my front door and wondered, "What's going on?".

Obviously wanting to rest, I refused to answer knowing that if it's urgent the knock will continue and that's exactly what happened. So I thought to myself, "What's going on?".

As I opened the door, I saw my 8-year-old son who said, "Mum, my sister had been knocked down by a car!"

She was my 9-year-old daughter who was accidentally killed by a car. The thought that came to me immediately was about the word of God I received previously to prepare me for the crisis to come and the voice of "Why me?" was silent for the Holy Spirit to take over.

Beloved, the word of God says that God will not allow you to be tempted more than what you can bear. Also, that our Sovereign Lord does nothing until He reveals His plans to His servants, the prophets.

Many things happen in life that we cannot understand, but what we should know, is what we know.

When we meet those who question situations in our lives that are not good, they ask, "What's going on?" followed by our own question of "Why me?".

When you receive the medical result you least expected and it is not good news, the next cause of action is for you to look at the doctor and ask the same question: "Why me?".

Beloved, life is full of mysteries.

Mysteries are things you cannot understand with the human mind. They are only revealed by the Spirit.

No wonder the Bible teaches us that **"The secret things belong to the Lord our God, but those things which are revealed belong to us and our children forever, that we may do all the words of the law" (Deuteronomy 29:29).**

"What's going on?" is the question for the unknown.

"What's going on?" is a question that requires an answer to what man cannot understand. The question is not the problem per se but the heart with which the question is asked!

Have you been asking that question lately or you are accustomed to asking such a question? Are you asking with the heart for a solution or asking to drown your innocence when you know you have done things wrong?

A typical example can be seen in the Bible; there was a king who sinned and had to face the consequence of his sin.

"At that time Abijah the son of Jeroboam became sick. And Jeroboam said to his wife, "Please arise, and disguise yourself, that they may not recognize you as the wife of Jeroboam, and go to Shiloh. Indeed, Ahijah the prophet is there, who told me that I would be king over this people. Also take with you ten loaves, some cakes, and a jar of honey, and go to him; he will tell you what will become of the child." And Jeroboam's wife did so; she arose and went to Shiloh, and came to the house of Ahijah. But Ahijah could not see, for his eyes were glazed by reason of his age.

Now the Lord had said to Ahijah, "Here is the wife of Jeroboam, coming to ask you something about her son, for he is sick. Thus and thus you shall say to her; for it will be, when she comes in, that she will pretend to be another woman."

And so it was, when Ahijah heard the sound of her footsteps as she came through the door, he said, "Come in, wife of Jeroboam. Why do you pretend to be another person? For I have been sent to you with bad news. Go, tell Jeroboam, 'Thus says the Lord God of Israel: "Because I exalted you from among the people, and made you ruler over My people Israel, and tore the kingdom away from the house of David, and gave it to you; and yet you have not been as My servant David, who kept My commandments and who followed Me with all his heart, to do only what was right in My eyes; but you have done more evil than all who were before you, for you have gone and made for yourself other gods and moulded images to provoke Me to anger, and have cast Me behind your back— therefore behold! I will bring disaster on the

house of Jeroboam, and will cut off from Jeroboam every male in Israel, bond and free; I will take away the remnant of the house of Jeroboam, as one takes away refuse until it is all gone" (1 Kings 14:1-10.. NKJV).

Jeroboam the King of Israel did evil in the sight of God and instead of him to repent of his wickedness he did not.

When his son was sick he sent his wife (the mother of the child) to ask the prophet what many of us usually ask our spiritual leader or directly to God: "What's going on with my family?", "What is going on with my business?", "What is wrong with my marriage?", "What is wrong with my health?" etc.

"What is wrong with me or what is going on?" is a common question.

We all want to be on top of situations in our lives but God deserves the right to make certain things unknown so we can ask Him for the unravelling of the mysteries.

The solution is not with a man but with God who reveals the answer to such questions.

Life is about "cause and effect"; "sowing and reaping".

Life is about "due process" and "due time".

We must go through the process of our making, and in the process of time God will come through to take the glory over our lives as He did for Joseph in the land of Egypt.

A million "What's wrong with me or why me?" could not have solved the problem of "due process" for Joseph.

Even David, the second King of Israel, went through the "due process" in life. Anointed to be king but was on the run from Saul the king for many years.

He could have asked "Why me?" for a thousand times from God but it would not have solved the problem.

The problem is not with the question of "What's going on?" but the motive for the question.

If we ask because we don't know, I believe we will get an answer at the appointed time. But if our motive is out of self-righteousness, as if we are well off and such crisis should not have happened, then we are to humble ourselves in repentance before God.

No man or woman deserves pain in life but we all go through pain for one reason or the other, especially when it is our choice that led to the crisis. Only repentance can solve the problem!

"What's going on?" and "Why me?" are all normal questions but we need to move into a purpose driven lifestyle to understand the positive aspect of such questions.

There is a purpose for every situation; for, God is not unjust in His dealings with men. He is righteous in all His ways, for sure.

Looking into the life of David is always interesting. He was not even his father's choice. He was not presented to Samuel, the prophet of God, when Jesse was asked to present his sons. The one the prophet even expected was rejected by God; David was chosen by God:

"And So Samuel did what the Lord said, and went to Bethlehem. And the elders of the town trembled at his coming, and said, "Do you come peaceably?" And he said "Peaceably; I have come to sacrifice to the Lord. Sanctify yourselves, and come with me to the sacrifice." Then he consecrated Jesse and his sons, and invited them to the sacrifice. So it was, when they came, that he looked at Eliab and said, "Surely the Lord's anointed is before him!" But the Lord said to Samuel, do not look at his appearance or at his physical stature, because I have refused him. For the Lord does not see as man sees, for man looks at the outward appearance, but the Lord looks at the heart" So Jesse called Abinadab, and made him pass before Samuel. And he said, "Neither has the Lord chosen this one. Then Jesse made Shammah pass by, and he said," Neither has the Lord chosen this one." Thus Jesse made seven of his sons pass before Samuel. And Samuel said to Jesse, "The Lord has not chosen these." And Samuel said to Jesse, "Are all the young men here? "Then he said. "There remains yet the youngest, and there he is, keeping sheep". And Samuel said to Jesse, "Send and bring him. For we will not sit down till he comes here." So he sent and brought him in. Now he was ruddy, with bright eyes, and good-looking. And the Lord said, "Arise, anoint him: for

this is the one!" Then Samuel took the horn of oil and anointed him in the midst of his brothers and the Spirit of the Lord came upon David from that day forward. So Samuel arose and went to Ramah" (1 Samuel 16:4-13).

David was neither the choice of his father nor Samuel but the choice of God. However, the process of making him rule as the anointed king over the nation was not an easy road. The stages of life he went through could have caused him to ask "What is going on?". And, maybe he did but the Bible is silent on such a scenario. We also do not read about him asking, "Why me?".

To suggest he never asked these two would have removed his humanity from him. All of us at a point in life have asked or will ask such questions; it all depends on where you are in your journey and the heart with which you ask such questions.

We tend to ask with amazement, "What is going on?" or we ask, "Why me?" when our expectation is not met or we encounter unexpected challenges in life.

Chapter Two
Fear Not

It is established that the word "fear not" appears in the Bible about 365 times so I, too, in agreement with the Scripture say to you "Fear not".

The word of God declares to us that **"God has not given us the spirit of fear but He has given unto us the Spirit of power, love and sound mind" (2 Timothy 1:7).**

You need to be bold in the Spirit because when you know who you are, you ask questions with the intention of having answers for a progressive lifestyle.

While growing up, my late father also taught me never to be afraid to ask questions with a motive of wanting to know and this is a lesson I am passing onto my children, readers and listeners, 'Never be afraid to ask questions.'

I encourage you to be like Bereans, **"These were more fair-minded or noble than those in Thessalonica in that they received the word with all readiness, and searched the Scriptures daily to find out whether these things were so" (Acts 17:11).** They were not afraid to search further to establish the truth of the Scriptures for themselves.

There are many things in life that expose us to fear. Yet the Scripture teaches us not to fear.

The fear of the unknown and what we will know when we search can sometimes bring fear to the mind of the weak.

The problem is not the question you often ask as I earlier pointed out to you, but the motive behind the question.

Asking questions with the right motive is good as it gives answers even though the answers may not be what we desire to hear.

Gideon asked the angel of the Lord, **"O my lord, if the Lord is with us, why then has all this happened to us? And where are all His miracles which our fathers told us about saying, 'Did not the Lord bring us up from Egypt? But now the Lord has forsaken us and delivered us into the hands of the Midianites"** (Judges 6:13).

The motive of Gideon's question was not anti-God but he asked as someone who wondered why there was not deliverance as heard of previously. Instead of being scolded by the angel of the Lord, he was commissioned to **"Go in this might of yours, and you shall save Israel from the hand of the Midianites. Have I not sent you? Judges 6:14.**

Oftentimes, what we questioned or ask about is the problem we are meant to solve. The question is the problem we are gifted, anointed and wired to solve.

Nehemiah asked his brethren who visited him three questions (Nehemiah 1:1-2).

Here are the questions:

- He asked the question concerning the Jews who had escaped.
- He asked the question about the ones who survived the captivity.
- He asked the question concerning Jerusalem.

"The words of Nehemiah the son of Hachaliah; It came to pass in the month of Chislev, in the twentieth year, as I was in Shushan the citadel, that Hanani one of my brethren came with men from Judah; and I asked them concerning the Jews who had escaped, who had survived the captivity and concerning Jerusalem" (Nehemiah 1:1-2).

The answers to these questions provoked his spirit to cry out to God in prayer: **"So it was, when I heard these words, that I sat down and wept, and mourned for many days; I was fasting and praying before the God of heaven"** (Nehemiah 1:4).

Nothing was wrong with the questions because he asked with a genuine concern about the welfare of his people. The answer given to him provoked a fruitful and favourable result.

Remember the question you ask exposes you to the problem you were created to solve... except if your motive for questioning others is of pride and not a sincere concern out of empathy.

As I have been emphasising all along, there is nothing wrong in asking questions, God wants us to ask so we can receive. Asking is not only in material things, **"Ask, and it will be given to you; seek and**

you will find, knock and it will be opened to you" (Matthew 7:7). God will never turn us back if we ask. So fear not.

In the days of Habakkuk, the prophet of God, he was grieved that despite his crying out to God for the state of the nation of Judah nothing seemed to be done by God to correct the situation. Prophet Habakkuk was not afraid to voice out his emotion to God. He was not afraid to let God know how he felt about the nation of Judah and his prayers that seemed unanswered.

"The burden which the prophet Habakkuk saw, O Lord, how long shall I cry, and You will not hear? Even cry out to You," violence!" and You will not save. Why do You show me iniquity, and cause me to see trouble? For plundering and violence are before me; there is strife and contention arises. Therefore the law is powerless and justice never goes forth, for the wicked surround the righteous therefore perverse judgement proceeds (Habakkuk 1:1-4).

Through our relationship with God we are to present our request to Him and wait for the answer. It may not be what you are prepared to hear but His answer will eventually gladden your heart if you trust Him at the end of the day.

Zechariah asked the angel who talked with him a question as well.

From the Scripture we read that Zechariah asked the angel who spoke to him questions for better understanding of what he saw in his vision. He asked "What are these?" in Zechariah 1:19. The angel too replied, **"These are the horns that have scattered Judah, Israel, and Jerusalem".**

To gain knowledge is to be an enquirer. In enquiring, you ask questions for clarification of matters.

Never be afraid of asking questions. Only ask to get a clarification of matters.

Fear is a tormentor for the Scripture says, **"There is no fear in love. But perfect love casts out fear, because fear involves torment. But he who fears has not been made perfect in love" (1John 4:18).**

Jesus said in the Scriptures, **"And do not fear those who kill the body but cannot kill the soul. But rather fear Him who is able to destroy both soul and body in hell" (Matthew 10:28).**

Whatever you do remember do not entertain fear in your mind, only reverence Christ with your life.

Job said, **"What I always feared has happened to me. What I dreaded has come true" (Job 3:25 New Living Translation).**

Fear has the ability to attract what you fear to you in the same way faith has the ability to attract victory and success to you. If fear rules your emotion and mind, defeat is guaranteed. Many die due to fear than stay alive by faith.

From the biblical account of Jesus walking on water, we see that Apostle Peter was not afraid to ask if it was He, Jesus, to bid him to come!

"Immediately Jesus made His disciples get into the boat and go before Him to the other side, while He sent the multitudes away. And when He had sent the multitudes away, He went up on the mountain by Himself to pray. Now when evening came, He was alone there. But the boat was now in the middle of the sea, tossed by the waves, for the wind was contrary.

Now in the fourth watch of the night Jesus went to them, walking on sea. And when the disciples saw Him walking on the sea, they were troubled, saying, "It is a ghost!" and they cried out for fear. But immediately Jesus spoke to them, saying, "Be of good cheer! It is I; do not be afraid". And Peter answered Him and said, "Lord, if it is You, command me to come to You on the water" (Matthew 14:22-28).

Here we read about fear factor that produced faith factor. Some of the disciples were afraid, thinking it was a ghost walking towards them on the sea. But Peter stepped out of fear and said, **"...if it is You, command me to come to You on the water"** (Matthew 14:28).

Never allow fear to stop your adventurous mind. If Peter never asked we would never know he could walk on water. But again when he lost sight of Jesus and turned to the boisterous wind, he began to sink till he cried out to Jesus saying, "Lord, save me." and he was saved.

"And immediately Jesus stretched out His hand and caught him, and said to him, "O you of little faith, why did you doubt?". And when they got into the boat, the wind ceased. Then those who were in the boat came and worshipped Him saying," Truly You are the Son of God" (Matthew 14:31-33).

Fear brings with it intimidation, but faith comes with boldness. Learn to step out of the "boat" and have an experience with Jesus.

Chapter Three
Why not you?

Often we ask "Why me?" to which I often say "Why not you?"

If something bad happens to anyone and the question of "Why me?" is raised, the question then is "Who would you want such to happen to?". When my daughter was killed by a motorist twenty seven years ago, because of the knowledge of this truth I'm imparting to my readers I wasn't at liberty to ask "Why me?". The reason being that before the event I knew I was going to face a satanic attack because of my purpose. I just did not know it was going to take the life of my firstborn on the road of London in the city and nation of my assignment. The process I had to go through was not planned by me but for me to cause me to know how awesome our God is! Please, I am not saying God killed my child of nine years old but I went through a divine process in time that made me to know that preaching is not just about theory but experiences born out fire! What the enemy meant for pain the good Lord meant it for my very good.

I was prepared against the satanic onslaught but I was not given the opportunity to know exactly how it would happen. Even, on the day of the accident I felt unusual in my spirit and I remembered I called her not to leave my Estate for the Estate opposite to which she said "Yes, Mummy." with a smile holding her brother and junior sister. But in less than 20mins I got a knock on my door about the accident from my 8 year-old son. By the time I got there with my husband (her father) she was dead! There were two paramedics' helicopters, several police cars and ambulance at the scene. It's the most horrible sight I have ever seen in my life as a mother.

I could not ask "Why me?". All I remembered I said was "Oh God!" at the memory of the prophetic word and the voice of the Holy Spirit that said "I am with you." just overwhemed me.

Now, you may wonder why I did not ask that question. It was because I already knew by the prophetic warning that I would go through fire.

Then you may say, "Why did you not pray against it?". My answer to that question was that all the prayer of Jesus couldn't stop His purpose of going to the Cross other than "Let your will be done.".

You see, beloved, there are things prayer will never change! Let that settle in your spirit right now. The teaching of "prayer answers everything literarily" is not true.

Prayer should align you to the will of God.

Prayer only sustains you or strengthens you to go through the fire and not be burnt. Prayer arranges each puzzle to fit into the full picture of life as ordained by God. God has a plan for our lives. A prayerful person can only pray the plan of God for their lives.

I went through fire but was not burnt because of God's promise **"When you pass through the waters, I will be with you; and through the rivers, they shall not overflow you, when you walk through the fire, you shall not be burned, nor shall the flame scorch you" (Isaiah 43:2).**

Before you ask "Why me?", can I ask you once again to count your blessings and name them one by one?

After Apostle Paul had his encounter on the road to Damascus, a man named Ananias was sent to pray for him.

"Now there was a certain disciple at Damascus named Ananias: and to him the Lord said in a vision, "Ananias" and he said, "Here I am, Lord". So the Lord said to him, arise and go to the street called Straight, and inquire at the house of Judas of one called Saul of Tarsus, for behold he is praying. And in a vision he has seen a man named Ananias coming in and putting his hand on him, so that he might receive his sight." Then Ananias answered, "Lord, I have heard from many about this man, how much harm he has done to Your saints in Jerusalem. And here he has authority from the chief priests to bind all who call on Your name. But the Lord said to him, "Go, for he is a chosen vessel of mine to bear my name before Gentiles, kings, and the children of Israel. For I will show him how many things he must suffer for my name's sake" (Acts 9:10-16).

With this message about Saul of Tarsus, no wonder he was willing to suffer many things for the sake of the gospel so that the name of Jesus could be heard accordingly. It was not a matter of asking "Why me?" for Saul, later called Paul but "Why not me?" when he wrote his epistle to the Galatians.

"But I make known to you, brethren that the gospel which was preached by me is not according to man. For I neither received it from man, nor was I taught it, but it came through the revelation of Jesus Christ. For you have heard of my former conduct in Judaism, how I persecuted the church of God beyond measure and tried to destroy it. And I advance in Judaism beyond many of my contemporaries in my own nation. Being more exceedingly zealous for the tradition of my fathers. But when it pleased God, who separated me from my mother's womb and called me through His grace, to reveal His Son in me, that I might preach Him among the Gentiles, I did not immediately confer with flesh and blood, nor did I go up to Jerusalem to those who were apostles before me; but I went to Arabia and return again to Damascus" (Galatians 1:11-17).

With this powerful account of Paul's encounter he was more grateful to be an apostle of Jesus hence he wrote the saints in Rome saying **"I am not ashamed of the gospel of Christ, for it is the power of God to salvation for everyone who believes for Jew first and also for the Greek. For in it the righteousness of God is revealed from faith to faith; as it is written "The just shall live by faith"** (Romans 1:16-17).

Remember the time you received an unexpected help from someone you never knew - why you?

The day you got your job rather than someone else interviewed for the same job, why you? If you are married, why you, when there are still many looking for a wife or a husband? When you went home with your baby from the labour room, why you? Have you forgotten there are several women still believing God? When you boarded that flight and landed safely, how many times did we hear about plane crashes but yours did not, why you? You still have a roof over your head but some have had their homes repossessed, why you with a roof over your head despite your income that hardly increases? Your children go to school or college and return home safe, why you? Which of them were you able to protect yourself? Count your blessings and ask why you with such blessings?

Life is full of mysteries. To witness some laughter while others are crying on the same matter is amazing. After the result of job interviews you hear someone rejoice while the others turn sad. So the question, "Why me?" can turn to "Why you?".

Any axe has two sides to its usefulness. Let us see the positive side of "Why me?" and fully appreciate God.

I am amazed at how King David was so grateful to God that one day he forgot himself and danced before his people while his wife Michal despised him in her heart.

"Then David returned to bless his household. And Michal the daughter of Saul came out to meet David, and said, "How glorious was the king of Israel today, uncovering himself today in the eyes of the maids of his servants, as one of the base fellows shamelessly uncover himself!

So David said to Michal, "It was before the Lord, who chose me instead of your father and all his house, to appoint me ruler over the people of the Lord, over Israel. Therefore I will play music before the Lord. And I will be even more undignified than this, and will be humble in my own sight. But as for the maidservants of whom you have spoken, by them I will be held in honour" (2 Samuel 6:20-22).

Be positive about "Why me?" so you can be lost in worship to God out of a heart of gratitude.

When you are grateful, you will see every situation as God lifting you rather than to complain or grumble because at the end of every dark tunnel is a glorious light that will shine.

Paul and Silas could have said "Why us?". They could have complained and grumbled against the jailer for beating them and throwing them in prison. But, at midnight, Paul and Silas began to pray and sang hymns to God, and the prisoners were listening to them. Suddenly, there was a great earthquake, so that the foundations of the prison were shaken; and, immediately, all the doors were opened and everyone's chains were loosed. (Acts. 16:25-26).

Instead of saying "Why me?" with a negative connotation see that it is a joyful experience to have to suffer for the cause of Christ.

Jesus said, **"Blessed are those who are persecuted for righteousness' sake, for theirs is the kingdom of Heaven" (Matthew 5:10).**

So when the enemy unleashes his plots against us as a result of our stand for Jesus, it is not the time to cry "Why me?" but to see it as a blessing. We have enough promises to assure us that we will go through many troubles but we should be of good cheers Jesus had overcome the world.

Peter in his epistle also said, **"Beloved, do not think it strange concerning the fiery trial which is to try you, as though some strange thing happened to you; but rejoice to the extent that you partake of Christ's sufferings, that when His glory is revealed, you may also be glad with exceeding joy" (1 Peter 4:12-13).**

So rejoice that you are a partaker of Christ's sufferings rather than wondering "Why me?".

Chapter Four
Go to the Potter's house

There are processes we must all go through.

"The word which came to Jeremiah from the Lord, saying: Arise and go down to the potter's house, and there I will cause you to hear My words."

Then the word of the Lord came to me, saying: "O house of Israel, can I not do with you as this potter?" says the Lord. Look, as the clay is in the potter's hand, so are you in my hand, O house of Israel!" (Jeremiah 18:1-2 & 5-6).

Since you and I are the work of God's Hand at creation we must also understand that His purpose for creating us cannot change.

We are like the clay in the hand of the Potter!

Firstly, know that the clay in the potter's hand was chosen from the rest of the clay.

You and I are chosen.

The word of God says that we are a chosen generation: **"But you are a chosen generation, a royal priesthood, a holy nation, His own special people, that you may proclaim the praises of Him who called you out of darkness into His marvellous light" (1 Peter 2:9).**

It's one thing to know that we were created in God's image and likenes, it's another thing to know we were not just spoken into existence like other created things according to the word of God in **Genesis 1:3-25: "Then God said, "Let there be light"; and there was light. And God saw the light that** *it was* **good; and God divided the light from the darkness. God called the light Day, and the darkness He called Night. So the evening and the morning were the first day.**

Then God said, "Let there be a firmament in the midst of the waters, and let it divide the waters from the waters." Thus God made the firmament, and divided the waters which *were* **under the firmament from the waters which** *were* **above the firmament; and it was so. And God called the firmament Heaven. So the evening and the morning were the second day.**

Then God said, "Let the waters under the heaven be gathered together into one place, and let the dry *land* **appear"; and it was so. And God called the dry** *land* **Earth, and the gathering together of the waters He called Seas. And God saw that it** *was* **good.**

Then God said, "Let the earth bring forth grass, the herb that yields seed, *and* **the fruit tree** *that* **yields fruit according to its kind, whose seed is in itself, on the earth"; and it was so. And the earth brought forth grass, and herb** *that* **yields seed according to its kind, and the tree that yields fruit, whose seed is according to its kind. And God saw that it** *was* **good. So the evening and the morning were the third day.**

Then God said, "Let there be lights in the firmament of the heaven to divide the day from the night; and let them be for signs and seasons, and for days and years; and let them be for lights

in the firmament of the heavens to give light on the earth"; and it was so. Then God made two great lights: the greater light to rule the day, and the lesser light to rule the night. *He made* the stars also. God set them in the firmament of the heaven to give light on the earth, and to rule over the day and over the night, and to divide the light from the darkness. And God saw that *it was* good. So the evening and the morning were the fourth day.

Then God said, "Let the waters abound with an abundance of living creatures, and let birds fly above the earth across the face of the firmament of heaven." So God created great sea creatures and every living thing that moves, with which the waters abounded, according to their kind, and every winged bird according to its kind. And God saw that *it was* good. And God blessed them, saying, "Be fruitful and multiply, and fill the waters in the seas, and let birds multiply on the earth." So the evening and the morning were the fifth day.

Then God said, "Let the earth bring forth the living creature according to its kind: cattle and creeping thing and beast of the earth, *each* according to its kind"; and it was so. And God made the beast of the earth according to its kind, cattle according to its kind, and everything that creeps on the earth according to its kind. And God saw that *it was* good."

But when it was time for humans to be made the statement became "Let Us make man", "Then God said, "Let Us make man in Our image, according to Our likeness; let them have dominion over the fish of the sea, over the birds of the air, and over the cattle, over all the earth and over every creeping thing that creeps on the earth." So God created man in His own image; in the image of God He created him; male and female He created them. Then God blessed them, and God said to them, "Be fruitful and multiply; fill the earth and subdue it; have dominion over the fish of the sea, over the birds of the air, and over every living thing that moves on the earth" (Genesis 1:26-28).

Beloved, if the creation of man has a purpose and process, I believe everything about humanity and God's plan for humanity has a process to it also: **"And the Lord formed man of the dust of the ground, and breathed into his nostrils the breath of life, and man became a living being" (Genesis 2:7).**

To present the first man Adam his companion, God took him through a process also.

"And the Lord God caused a deep sleep to fall on Adam, and he slept; and He took one of his ribs, and closed up the flesh in its place. Then the rib which the Lord God had taken from man He made into a woman, and He brought her to the man.
And Adam said:
"This is now bone of my bones
And flesh of my flesh;
She shall be called Woman,
Because she was taken out of Man."
Therefore a man shall leave his father and mother and be joined to his wife, and they shall become one flesh.
And they were both naked, the man and his wife, and were

not ashamed" (Genesis 2:21-25).

Everything God made, He made through His ordained process. So also our becoming His dream on earth is through a process.

From the conception to the birth of a child is a process. From our childhood to adulthood we go through a process. Each developmental stage is checked to be sure the process of growth is complete.

The plant, animal, bird and fish too go through a process.

The process of planting is different from the mating season of animals. It is different to the birds and fish with their process of laying eggs to hatching of eggs. These all go through different processes.

So what is Process?

It is a series of actions or operations to achieve an end goal. There are series of actions or operations in life that we cannot avoid in order to become who God says we are: to become like Jesus, successful business men and women, the best and our dream.

After all, Isaac **BEGAN** to prosper; he **CONTINUED** to prosper till he **BECAME** a prosperous man (Genesis 26:13). These are three different stages that involve different processes and "due time".

So, beloved, with this understanding, do not run from your process, rather co-operate with the process of God in making you His beloved on earth.

Secondly, looking at the potter and the clay on the wheel is amazing. It is a place of shaping the clay to the design the potter has in mind. When the word says that we are a royal priesthood, it's more than words. We were not born naturally as a royal priesthood. We received that through our redemptive nature, a new life. The process of shaping us to live, walk and talk like one starts from the moment we received Jesus as our risen Saviour and submit to Him as Lord. This process begins in our MIND! The Word says that that's who we are but the mind says, 'No'. So the word of God is the instrument on the wheel to shape our mind to conform to the truth.

The shaping of the design is on the wheel; do you ever feel like your life is going in a circle? Maybe you are on "the wheel" of the Potter for a better shape of you.

After the shape, there's a dry season in the sun wherein you may feel as if everyone is ignoring you or walking past you, or you are left behind others but that forgetting you are in a process. No one is ever left behind until after Rapture when those who will not go are the real "left behind" beloved.

Everything in our natural self is rough and crude. And there is a time for rough edges to be smoothed like those difficult and rough times in relationships when brethren through frictions would bring the best out of you,

Proverbs 27:17 says "As iron sharpens iron, so a man sharpens the countenance of his friend".

The iron given to sharpen you is not always nice. It is not what you expected but it is necessary for your rough edges to become smooth. During the process to get to the end result as ordained by God, there is a time for intense application of heat to solidify the clay from cracking easily. Going through fire in life is a normal process. To eat some meals, you must apply fire. To get pure gold you need fire. To be a producer of usable products, fire is useful.

To all believers I want you to know that we have the promise of our God from the book of Prophet Isaiah 43:2 which says, **"When you pass through the waters, *I will* be with you; And through the rivers, they shall not overflow you. When you walk through the fire, you shall not be burned, nor shall the flame scorch you."**

No matter the heat used to purify gold, gold always comes out pure. There is heat that destroys and heat that purifies. To go through the potter's house the fire is not to destroy but to solidify and purify. We always see the end result in the 'For Sale' shop or on display to beautify our homes but no one knows the full extent of the process in the Potter's house. We are clay in the hand of the Potter. No matter how many times the clay cries, complains, grumbles, it would not stop the process of making the clay what the potter set out to achieve.

I pray you will fully submit to God's process. It is possible by grace.

During the process of becoming what you aspire to be to glorify God, asking "What's going on?" or "Why me?", your motivation for asking such questions should be because you desire understanding and truly understanding will be given to you.

Unfortunately, this is the time we tend to look at others and start comparing ourselves with those around us. At this point, I want you to know that just because your friends seem to be having promotion at work and you are still on the same position or they are changing their cars while you are still driving the same for years or going on family holiday while you are struggling to pay your rent does not mean that God has forgotten you or you are not progressing.

This is not the time to be asking "Why me?".

Please note, I am encouraging you to look beyond the natural and look to heaven where your help comes from.

Psalm 121: 1-8 declares "I will lift up my eyes to the hills- From whence comes my help? My help *comes* from the Lord, Who made heaven and earth. He will not allow your foot to be moved; He who keeps you will not slumber. Behold He who keeps Israel, Shall neither slumber nor sleep. The Lord *is* your keeper; The Lord is your shade at your right hand. The sun shall not strike you by day or the moon by night. The Lord shall preserve you from all evil; He shall preserve your soul. The Lord shall preserve your going out and your coming in from this time forth and even forevermore".

For everyone there is time and season. Your testimony is already sealed in Christ.

Joseph had a dream at seventeen years of age and shared the dream with his brothers and father according to Genesis 37:2-11.

"This *is* the history of Jacob. Joseph, *being* seventeen years old, was feeding the flock with his brothers. And the lad *was* with the sons of Bilhah and the sons of Zilpah, his father's wives; and Joseph brought a bad report of them to his father. Now Israel loved Joseph more than all his children, because he *was* the son of his old age. Also he made him a tunic of *many* colours. But when his brothers saw that their father loved him more than all his brothers, they hated him and could not speak peaceably to him.

Now Joseph had a dream, and he told *it* to his brothers; and they hated him even more. So he said to them, "Please hear this dream which I have dreamed: There we were, binding sheaves in the field. Then behold, my sheaf arose and also stood upright; and indeed your sheaves stood all around and bowed down to my sheaf." And his brothers said to him, "Shall you indeed reign over us? Or shall you indeed have dominion over us?" So they hated him even more for his dreams and for his words. Then he dreamed still another dream and told it to his brothers, and said, "Look, I have dreamed another dream. And this time, the sun, the moon, and the eleven stars bowed down to me." So he told it to his father and his brothers; and his father rebuked him and said to him, "What is this dream that you have dreamed? Shall your mother and I and your brothers indeed come to bow down to the earth

before you?" And his brothers envied him, but his father kept the matter *in mind*"

Joseph probably said to himself "Why me?". Nobody knows since the Scripture does not record such; it is just this writer's thought. But for sharing his dream he ended up in Egypt as a slave, a slave in service but with his dream still within him.

Joseph the dreamer ended up as a slave and a prisoner but God was with him throughout his ordeal. **"The Lord was with Joseph, and he was a successful man; and he was in the house of his master the Egyptian" (Genesis 39:2).**

Even though God was with him, his master's wife lied against him for not refusing to lie with her: **"And it came to pass after these things that his master's wife cast longing eyes on Joseph, and she said, "Lie with me" (Genesis 39:7).**

For refusing to lie with her, Joseph was thrown in jail but his dream was still inside of him. While he interpreted other people's dreams it seemed as if his dream was not interpreted. These crises were enough to cause him to lose sight of God and became a bitter man. All these were enough for Joseph to have lost focus of who God is and even kill himself. After all, "What is the use of living?" as many have said in their moment of despair. Yet Joseph kept himself pure before God.

While in prison, the keeper of prison committed to Joseph all the prisoners in prison; whatever they did was Joseph doing. **"The keeper of the prison did not look into anything that was under Joseph's authority, because the Lord was with him; and whatever he did, the Lord made it to prosper"** (Genesis 39:23).

Where are you at the moment?

Is your life right now like that of Joseph?

All because some of your family members see you as a prominent child or your friends see you as head and shoulder above them they plotted your fall or kicked you out of family inheritance.

Remember, it is not over.

God is still with you. Stop asking, "Why me?". Count your blessings.

First blessing is that you are still alive in the hand of the Potter. Your dream is still intact and God is still with you. Do not give up on God. When your time comes for manifestation of God's glory to be made known, your blessings will be to the glory of God.

Chapter Five
Exposing pride in our heart

Pride is deep.

Pride is the inward belief that you are better than others and this belief is outwardly demonstrated when we believe that we are not supposed to have challenges simply because we are better than others.

Pride is spiritual because it denies the word of God the process of maturing us through what we go through. It denies what Jesus said that in this world we will have many troubles but we should be of good cheers; for, we have overcome the world.

Pride begins as a thought. As the Bible says, "As a man thinks in his heart so is he" (Proverbs 23:7). If you think that as a result of your prayer life or your giving to God or your ministry you should not have challenges or problems, you are proud. To make yourself believe you are superior to others and above negative circumstances of life is definitely pride.

As a matter of fact, your prayer life does not make you immune to the challenges of life; instead, it helps you see them as God sees them. It raises the bar of vision to see God bigger than all the mountains and helps you speak to mountains to move by faith.

Note that God "resists the proud but gives grace to the humble".

Pride cost Lucifer to fall.

Isaiah 14:12-15 says, **"How you are fallen from heaven. O Lucifer, son of the morning. How you are cut down to the ground, you who weakened the nations!**

For you have said in your heart, I will ascend into heaven, I will exalt my throne above the stars of God; I will also sit on the mount of the congregation on the farthest sides, of the north; I will ascend above the heights of the clouds, I will be like the Most High'. Yet you shall be brought down to Sheol, to the lowest depths of the Pit."

Pride is like sexual sin. There are deep issues within.

Concerning sexual sin, Jesus said that **"You have heard that it was said to those of old 'You shall not commit adultery.' But I say to you that whoever looks at a woman to lust for her has already committed adultery with her in his heart"** (Matthew 5:27-28).

As pride is within you, so is sexual sin within you and when sexual sin is committed, it is pride within that hinders a man or woman from admitting and confessing it and thereby denying mercy and deliverance that can be received.

Having a quiet nature is not a sign of humility! A man or woman can be an introvert and still be proud. While an extrovert is often perceived to be arrogant even though they may be humble. Pride is not to be confused with the way a man or woman is wired. It can be deceitfully employed within a man or woman. It takes the word of God and the work of the Holy Spirit to expose pride!

Understand this: if Lucifer was sent out of heaven because of pride, no one can abide in the presence of God with a prideful heart without repenting.

The word of God says, **"God resists the proud, but gives grace to the humble" (James 4:6).**

So asking "Why me?" with a mind-set that you are better than others or believing that you deserve more than what you have without being grateful is pride; it only exposes your ailing heart and further brings you into resistance from the grace of God.

Pride is subtle; you can be deceived thinking you are not proud even though you are. Eliab (David's senior brother) was proud yet accused David of pride.

"Now his oldest brother heard when he spoke to the men; and Eliab's anger was aroused against David, and he said, "Why did you come down here? And with whom have you left those few sheep in the wilderness? I know your pride and the insolence of your heart, for you have come down to see the battle" (1 Samuel 17:28).

Having an enquiring mind is not the problem here but the response is! Enquiring with the goal of being a solution to the problem is not pride.

Chapter Six
Danger of anxiety

It has been said that anxiety is an experience one has at a point in life. For some it is a daily occurrence but for others, it is a stronghold that is needed to be destroyed. 'The yoke shall be destroyed by reason of the anointing.' says the Bible.

The Bible says, **"Be anxious for nothing, but in everything by prayer and supplication, with thanksgiving, let your requests be made known to God; and the peace of God, which surpasses all understanding, will guard your hearts and minds through Christ Jesus" (Philippians 4:6-7).**

We are leaving in a time where anxiety is dominating the mind of many. What was secure is no longer secure, and several people have been affected by the present global pandemic.

As a follower of Jesus, when events seem negative, never ask "Why me?" because God has a plan for your life. God has said, **"For I know the thoughts that I think toward you, says the Lord, thoughts of peace and not of evil, to give you a future and a hope" (Jeremiah 29:11).**

He also said, **"For My thoughts are not your thoughts, nor are your ways My ways," says the Lord. For as the heavens are higher than the earth, so are My ways higher than your ways and My thoughts than your thoughts" (Isaiah 55:8-9).**

What is needed is a revelation of God's intended purpose for allowing us to go through the situations we find ourselves, and for us to pray and inquire what we are to do in our season.

Anxiety will dangerously affect your emotion, your mind and in turn affect your health. Through your devotion to Christ, I pray you gain insight into His will for your life and His intended purpose for every situation that confronts you.

Also, there are times we do not know but we still have to trust God by faith, knowing He has our best interest at heart; after all, the Bible says, **"He who did not spare His own Son, but delivered Him up for us all, how shall He not with Him also freely give us all things?" (Romans 8:32).**

Chapter Seven

I am fearfully and wonderfully made

One of the Scriptures that helped me value myself as a young follower of Jesus Christ 34 years ago is found in Psalm 139:14 (NKJV) which says, **"I will praise You, for I am fearfully and wonderfully made; marvellous are Your works, and that my soul knows very well."**

The Passion Translation (TPT) says, **"I thank you God, for making me so mysteriously complex! Everything you do is marvellous breath-taking. It simply amazes me to think about it! How thoroughly you know me, Lord."**

When you understand who you are, you will know that God has your back.

In the beginning God said, **"Let Us make man in our image, according to Our likeness; let them have dominion over the fish of the sea, over the birds of the air, and over the cattle, over all the earth and over every creeping thing that creeps on the earth. So God created man in His own image; in the image of God He created him; male and female He created them. Then God blesses them, and God said to them, "Be fruitful, and multiply; fill the earth and subdue it; have dominion over the fish of the sea, over the birds of the air, and over every living thing that moves on the earth"** (Genesis 1:26-28).

With the knowledge of how you and I came into being, how then can we conceive it in our minds that we are forgotten by God because of challenges of life or that we are defeated because of tough times? It is a sign of unbelief and may God help your unbelief. Know the

I AM FEARFULLY AND WONDERFULLY MADE

Scripture which says: **"Knowing that you were not redeemed with corruptible things, like silver or gold, from your aimless conduct received by tradition from your fathers, but by the precious blood of Christ, as of a lamb without blemish and without spot. He indeed was foreordained before the foundation of the world, but was manifest in these last times for you who through Him believe in God, who raised Him from the dead and gave Him glory so that your faith and hope are in God"** (1 Peter 1:18-21).

God can neither forget you nor forsake you in times of trouble because He promised never to leave us nor forsake us.

The word of God further states that **"And we know that all things work together for good to those who love God, to those who are the called according to His purpose. For whom He foreknew, He also predestined to be conformed to the image of His Son, that He might be the firstborn among many brethren. Moreover, who He predestined, these He also called, whom He called, these He also justified, and whom He justified, these He also glorified. What then shall we say to these things? If God is for us, who can be against us? He who did not spare His own Son, but delivered Him up for us all, how shall He not with Him also freely give us all things?** (Romans 8:28-32).

I want you to know and understand that you are fearfully, delicately, marvellously, and wonderfully made. Not only are you made in such a manner, but as a follower of Jesus Christ the Son of God, you are redeemed and justified by the precious blood of Jesus.

God saw that sin corrupted the first gene so he fixed it by sending us His only begotten Son - Jesus. Through Christ we have victory over sin and death. His Blood atoned for our sins, and His divine power has given us all things that pertain to life and godliness, through the knowledge of Him who called us by His glory and virtue. (2 Peter 1:3)

Now, we are sons of God. We are heirs of the Father; we are joint heirs with the Son. We are children of the Kingdom of Light. We are in God's Family.

For God not to spare His own Son, but delivered Him up for us all, how shall He not with Him also freely give us all things? (Romans 8:32).

Now, see why it is you who qualified to go through the process because of purpose and the Father's love!

At this point, you should shout 'Hallelujah!'

You should rejoice and be glad. The point is that when you know who you are, you will not ask "Why me?" with a negative undertone but you will rejoice in the knowing that the uncomfortable situation will work together for your good because you love the Lord.

Chapter Eight
Myth-life is smooth...isn't it?

There is this belief that once you turn your life to Jesus all your challenges disappear. I do not know where this belief came from but some of us question God at every crisis point; we fail to see Him in the midst of fire as our number four Man (Daniel 3:23-26). We fail to understand that the presence of sin in the world has produced a life of pain and sweat: **"Man who is born of woman is of few days and full of trouble" (Job 14:1).**

The Scripture also teaches us that many are the afflictions of the righteous but the Lord delivers him out of them all (Psalm 34:19).

Even Jesus said, **"These things I have spoken to you, that in Me you may have peace. In the world you will have tribulation; but be of good cheer, I have overcome the world" (John 16:33).**

From these three Scriptures it is clear that life is definitely full of trouble; there is no smooth ride.

You do not need to look for trouble, trouble is here! Right from the womb we prevailed over trouble. Out of the billions of sperms released you out-ran the rest to hit the egg from your mother's womb. There was trouble from the moment you showed up on earth: trouble in school and in every corner you turned to while growing up but yet these troubles did not overcome you and will never defeat you because of the promise that says you are an overcomer.

"For whatever is born of God overcomes the world. And this is the victory that has overcome the world – our faith." (1 John 5:4).

So, my brethren, take courage knowing that whatever you are going through will not defeat you.

You are born to win.

Asking "Why me?" in the midst of crisis is not the solution to the crisis but understanding the heart of God for the crisis is important.

According to the Scripture in Amos 3:7, our God will not do anything until He first reveals to His servants the prophets.

I have come to know that God always gives us a sign or signs but we often ignore or not discern the signs before trouble sets in. But righteous God still steps in to turn things around for our good to those who love Him in the end.

You are more than a conqueror through Jesus Christ our Lord. All your doubts and anxieties are agents from the kingdom of darkness to bring you to a place of defeat but I dare you to believe God! I dare you to trust Him who did not spare His only begotten Son from dying for you when you were deep in sin! How much more now that you have crossed from darkness to His marvellous light will He abandon you! God forbid!

Chapter Nine
Turn of events

There is always a moment that events of life take a new turn. Do you know that many give up at the moment their life story is about to change?

There is always a turn of events in each person's life. Never give up! Do not allow your "Why me?" question to drown the voice that encourages you to look up to where your help comes from. Your help comes from the Lord, the Maker of the Heavens and the Earth.

The turn of events in Joseph's life came when Pharaoh dreamt and no one could interpret his dream. It was at that moment that the butler remembered his fault.

"Then the chief butler spoke to Pharaoh, saying: "I remember my faults this day" (Genesis 41:9).

On hearing about Joseph, Pharaoh immediately sent for him. He did not give up because the butler forgot him in prison. The dream of the king of Egypt caused a dramatic turn of events for Joseph. I declare a turn of events happening over your life right now!

Hold on!

Your condition is about to change and you will sing a new song in the land of the living.

For forty days, morning and evening Goliath taunted Israel. Suddenly events took a dramatic turn when Jesse sent His Son, David, to go and give food to his brothers in the battlefield and see how they fared so David could bring news back to him.

"And the Philistine drew near and presented himself forty days, morning and evening. Then Jesse said to his son David, "Take now for your brothers an ephah of this dried *grain* and these ten loaves, and run to your brothers at the camp. And carry these ten cheeses to the captain of *their* thousand, and see how your brothers fare, and bring back news of them" (1 Samuel 17:16-18).

It was in the Valley of Ella that Goliath was defeated by David and his story changed forever. May your story change for good today!

When your story is to change, events in your life will change or take a new turn. It could be a change in government or a change in position or location. Many things can happen to cause a turn of events but whatever it is, get ready. Do not be caught unawares!

We are in the pandemic now. Many people have come into their turn for good as a result of the pandemic while some entered moments of grief.

I pray you learn to recognise which season you are in and never give up.

Chapter Ten
Encouragement is necessary but....

We all need encouragement in life but what happens when those you expect encouragement from do not encourage you but turn against you?

What happens when in your moment of pain those who are supposed to encourage you, those you expect to help hold you steady and not give up are the very ones who speak like Job's friends in **Job 42:7, "And so it was, after the Lord had spoken these words to Job, that the Lord said to Eliphaz the Temanite, " My wrath is aroused against you and your two friends, for you have not spoken of Me what is right, as My servant Job has."**

Their words were of no pity, causing Job to say, **"I have heard many such things; miserable comforters are you all!" (Job 16:2).** Oh! There are several miserable comforters around! Life is full of them.

With friends described as miserable comforters you don't need enemies; you already got them. But then what do you do when those who are to encourage you turn against you?

May I challenge you at this point to encourage yourself in the Lord still.

David at a point in his life was faced with discouraged men as if he was not discouraged himself. Instead of turning against his men or dwelling in discouragement this is what the Bible records, **"Now David was greatly distressed, for the people spoke of stoning him because the soul of all the people was grieved, every man for his sons and daughters. But David strengthened himself in the Lord**

his God" (1 Samuel 30:6).

When all is against you and life throws many challenges, when loved ones turn against you despite doing your best but it is never good enough, learn to do what David did. Turn to the Lord and strengthen yourself in Him by recounting the good old days and singing His praises.

Also, wait on the Lord for a strategy on what to do to regain your lost ground. Battles are never won by weapons but by strategies.

The process David pursued was: he sought the Lord. **"David inquired of the Lord, saying. Shall I pursue this troop? Shall I overtake them?" (1 Samuel 30:8).**

Always seek the Lord for solutions and never assume you know what to do because there is a way that appears to be right, but in the end it leads to death (Proverbs 14:12). The best we know to do in crisis may not bring the desired plan of God for our lives; after all, God must be glorified in all of our lives.

He waited for the answer and God answered him.

"And He answered him. "Pursue, for you shall surely overtake them and without fail recover all" (1 Samuel 30:8).

There is a place to consult man for counsel and there is a place for you to know that only God can give you what men cannot give you, which is, a strategy for victory and success.

There is a positive aspect to the question too...

Be the director of your future scripts. Instead of seating down sorrowfully asking questions with answers that your mind is not even ready to receive, never stop praying and believing in the miracle-working God. Oh yes! This may be challenging but as long as it's not difficult for you to breathe never let it be difficult for you to talk to God.

Also remember, in the good times you have testified to the goodness of the Lord. Remember Job did not deny God as his wife suggested but kept his integrity (Job 2:9). It is better to keep your integrity than to deny God in times of trouble. It is even better to remain silent than to speak what you will regret later. Weigh your words before you say them. It can encourage or discourage, build or destroy, root out or plant. Words are powerful and actions are important in the course of life.

Learn to speak words of faith. Speak positively into your life no matter what. Let no corrupt communication come out of your mouth. Remember, today is not tomorrow. Yesterday is gone, today is definitely a gift for you. Your future is in the Hand of God. He knows the thought that He thinks towards you, thoughts of peace and not of evil, to give you a future and a hope (Jeremiah 29:11).

Refuse to be discouraged regardless of your challenges; you have what it takes to encourage yourself in the Lord.

The Apostles and the early Church in Jerusalem had a disciple whose name was Barnabas, translated to mean "son of encouragement". He was a Levite of the country of Cyprus, having land; he sold it, and brought the money and laid it at the Apostles' feet.

You also can choose to be a 'son of encouragement' to others by your words and actions.

Chapter Eleven

Born to win....Born to rule

"For whatever is born of God overcomes the world and this is the victory that has overcome the world - our faith. Who is he who overcomes the world, he who believes that Jesus is the Son of God" (1 John 5:4-5).

I want you to know that you were not born to be defeated. You were not born to lose a battle because in Jesus Christ we have the victory.

Our position in Christ is secured, as the Bible says in Ephesians 1:20-23 that we are raised with Him and seated at the right Hand of God in the heavenly places, far above all principality and power and might and dominion, and every name that is named, not only in this age but also in that which is to come. And He put all things under His feet, and gave Him to be the head over all things to the church, which is His body, the fullness of Him who fills all in all.

According to our position in Jesus Christ we are born to win and rule.

Your victory is in the knowledge of who you are and knowing your position in Him. When you know and understand these two truths, you will walk confidently on the road to victory, knowing that He who will come, will come and will not tarry over your case.

The lesson of life is that you cannot get to your glory land without your stories to tell. To arrive at Canaan Land there are various stages to pass through.

Chapter Twelve

Next step...

Start praising God like you mean it. Be like Paul and Silas who sang in prison before they were released: **"But at midnight Paul and Silas were praying and singing hymns to God, and the prisoners were listening to them. Suddenly there was a great earthquake, so that the foundations of the prison were shaken; and immediately all the doors were opened and everyone's chains were loosed."** (Acts 16:25-26).

Do not wait till the situation changes for good; start now! Paul and Silas did not wait until the jailer set them free; they sang at midnight.

Where you are right now is your midnight; start singing and see how wonders will happen.

Conclusion:

Turn your *"Why me?"* into *"Why not me?"* and count your blessings.

ORDINATION

A LICENCE TO DIE BEFORE YOU LIVE

LOLA OYEBADE

LOLA OYEBADE

Fulfilling
HIS
Dream

Experience A Life Of Possibilities
Through Grace